50%

OFF!

HOW TO FIND GREAT DEALS

Todd Holze & Duane Holze

This book is available at a special discount when ordered in bulk quantities. For information, contact TLC Publishing.

Published by
TLC Publishing
P.O. Box 8246
New Fairfield, CT 06812

Library of Congress Catalog Card Number: 99-90281
ISBN: 0-9671-5010-8
Printed in the United States of America

This publication is designed to be an educational and informative guide with regard to the subject matter. The advice and strategies presented in this book should be used as a guide and not be relied upon as a substitute for the reader's own common sense and good judgment. The authors, publisher or distributor, individually or cooperatively, do not accept responsibility for any liabilities or other problems that may develop from following these guidelines. The author, publisher or distributor is not engaged in rendering any legal or other professional advice. If legal or other professional assistance is required, the services of a competent professional should be sought.

Table of Contents

Preface

Imagine a lifestyle full of everything you have always wanted, on your current salary! Would you like to come home and relax in the hot tub after a hard day at work or have the extra money to take that dream vacation? Congratulations! You are holding the book that can help you accomplish these things and so much more.

Through the years we learned to appreciate the wealth of opportunity available in the used market. As we developed the principles for success described in this book, the deals we made became bigger and better. Our friends and relatives were amazed and would laugh with astonishment while asking, "How do you find these deals?" or "Can you help me get a deal on what I need?" Before long, we were giving lessons on where to look, what to ask and how to negotiate.

Friends of ours, who would never have considered buying pre-owned merchandise, began to realize how much money they could save by shopping in the used market. After their first purchase, they were hooked! We were constantly helping friends and relatives find deals to save money. It was then we realized that there are so many people who would like to be doing the same thing.

This book was designed and written to provide the information you need to start saving money today in the used market. You can begin buying items at below fair market price with very little effort. How do you get started? What do you look for? Where do you find these deals? All of these questions and more are answered in this book.

The opportunity for success is waiting. Congratulations! You are on your way to the ultimate buying power.

"Buying More and Paying Less."

The Advantages

50% HUMOR

It's funny half the time!

FOR SALE: Fish tank, 30 gallon, complete except for fish, $75. Also FREE, 1 Siamese cat, likes fishing.

FOR SALE: Complete set of Encyclopedias, excellent condition, $75, no longer needed. Got married last weekend, wife knows everything.

FOR SALE: Washer & dryer, $200, must sell, moving to nudist colony.

HOUSE FOR SALE: 4BR, 2 1/2 BTH, mother/daughter style, mother included.

FOR SALE: Car alarm system, complete, $300, didn't have the chance to install.

The used market can offer enormous benefits to the average consumer. By simply applying the techniques in this book, you can literally save thousands of dollars on the items you use every day. Here are just some of the many advantages you can look forward to experiencing.

SAVE BIG $$$

It's no secret! The most obvious advantage of buying preowned merchandise is the ability to buy at a fraction of the new cost. Take the example of furnishing a new home or apartment. Purchases could include a washer, dryer, refrigerator, freezer, bedroom set, living room furniture, lawnmower or tractor, yard tools, patio furniture, and the list goes on and on. The costs can be astronomical if everything is bought brand new. But buy those same items in the used market and you can put the savings in your pocket.

COMPARE AND SAVE
Compare the new costs to the quality preowned costs of all the durable goods you will purchase in a lifetime and you will find the difference is staggering.

These savings are available on almost every durable good. You can repeatedly purchase items at discounted prices, sometimes never used and still under warranty. Deals like this are everywhere and this book can show you where and how to find them.

Avoid the "Hidden Costs"

If the sticker price on your last new purchase didn't shock you, how about the hidden costs? Additional fees such as sales tax, preparation, assembly and delivery fees are just some of the unavoidable costs on almost every new item, adding considerably more to the purchase price.

Hidden costs include the fees you pay to have a dealer register a car, furniture delivered to your door or a new bicycle assembled. Because many manufacturers ship their products disassembled to reduce costs, department stores add a fee to the price tag for the cost of assembly.

> ### GREAT DEALS
> The used market is full of financial and emotional rewards. Take advantage of the opportunities.

Consumers pay these types of hidden costs time and time again. If you ask most people what they paid for a product, they remember the amount on the price tag and not the final price listed on the receipt. By buying through the used market, most of these fees can be avoided.

UPGRADE OR CHANGE STYLES

How often do you grow tired of the styles in your home, but do not upgrade due to the costs? By buying a preowned item, you can afford to upgrade to a newer model or style at anytime. It's a way of life that can save you thousands of dollars.

> **BEST BUYS**
> Wouldn't it be great to buy all of your major goods at a discount rate? Better yet, wouldn't you like to sell those items years later for the same price or more? It's all possible in the used market.

BUILD CONFIDENCE

The strategies in this book will help you build the confidence needed to negotiate effectively. As your confidence level builds, you will reinforce your negotiating skills. This process becomes an ongoing cycle of improvement.

There is something rewarding, both emotionally and financially, when you negotiate a good deal and save money. Most people gain a sense of pride from knowing they own the items rather than having to make scheduled payments. Discover the rewards and excitement as you learn the techniques you need to acquire "Great Deals."

Product
Life Cycle

50% HUMOR

It's funny half the time!

YOU KNOW IT'S TIME TO UPGRADE WHEN:

- Your auto mechanic sends a get well card addressed to your car
- The Maytag repairman is on speed dial
- The magnets on the refrigerator are holding on the door
- The snow blower only starts in the summer
- Your employer asks you to park in the back as to not deter customers
- Duct tape is the main tool used for repairs

REASONS TO CLEAN THE GARAGE:

- With all the mess, you forgot you had one
- The dog has been missing for three weeks
- You can't find the car
- It's golf season and your clubs are missing
- You need a last minute birthday gift

CHAPTER

Imagine selling items you have purchased for the same price as you originally paid or even more! It's a simple procedure illustrated by the "Product Life Cycle" map for success. This method can be used to minimize depreciation, acquire free use of merchandise and even make a profit on the resale.

In your lifetime the goods you purchase will wear out, go out of style or you may simply grow tired of them. But commonly,

"UH OH, IT BROKE"
Things can break down at the most inopportune time. Don't wait until an item fails to replace it.

people keep things long after the point at which they could recover their investment. For some it is because they become emotionally attached to material items. Others may keep the working item because they think the replacement cost would be too high.

How many times has a breakdown occurred at the most inopportune time? Just when you need the item most, it stops working. It's called the "Uh oh, it broke" syndrome. Many people avoid the problem until it's too late. But with a little planning and an understanding of the Product Life Cycle, these problems can be avoided.

A brand new product may have a long life, but it is practically impossible to get the initial purchase price back on the resale regardless of its condition. Like a new automobile, once you drive it off the lot, it is unlikely to be resold for the original price. This chapter will show you an alternative to this kind of financial loss.

PRODUCT LIFE CYCLE

The Product Life Cycle is the useful life of a durable good. These are items or goods with a relatively long life like furniture, appliances, cars, boats, lawn equipment, recreational items and so on.

DEPRECIATION
The maximum rate of depreciation occurs just after the initial purchase. By buying a preowned product you can avoid this financial loss.

From the time an item is purchased until the time it is thrown away, the product goes through a series of phases in which the value of the item will decrease or depreciate. However, an item has a higher rate of depreciation in the beginning of its life than towards the end. The graph in Figure 2.1 shows the phases a product will go through during the course of its life. Let's discuss them in more detail.

STICKER SHOCK AND THE HIDDEN COSTS

Check your receipt on almost any new purchase and its obvious that the price you paid is not the price on the sticker. There are always additional hidden costs associated with buying a new

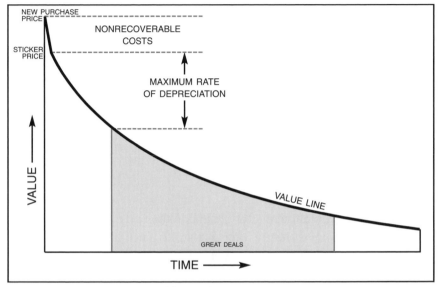

Figure 2.1 The Product Life Cycle

item: sales tax, delivery costs, finder's fees, commissions, assembly fees or preparation fees. These costs can add substantially more to the price tag.

However, after the purchase these additional costs do not add to the overall value of the item. The resale value is still only the price on the sticker or in most cases, far less. These hidden costs, commonly referred to as nonrecoverable costs, are not recovered when selling the item.

LET DEPRECIATION WORK FOR YOU

From the time a durable good is purchased, it begins to depreciate, losing value every day. Although depreciation occurs over the entire life of the product, the greatest rate of depreciation occurs just after the initial purchase. This can be anywhere from a day to several years depending on the type of product.

Some products will hold their value better than others will. For example, a computer can depreciate in a matter of months while a car may take several years to reach the same percentage of loss. By buying a preowned product you can avoid the initial depreciation and achieve big savings.

GREAT DEALS

The best deals are found after the maximum rate of depreciation. It is at this time or shortly after that an item can be bought for a bargain price. The depreciation curve (value line) begins to level off, leaving you the opportunity to use the item with minimal cost and maintain a good resale value. It is such an important time in the Product Life Cycle that we will discuss it in greater detail shortly.

INCREASED MAINTENANCE

There comes a point when products can be a nightmare to own. The product continues to deteriorate and show signs of wear, needed repairs escalate and maintenance costs begin to increase while the value continually depreciates. You do not want to own a product at this time.

It can be a very frustrating time to own the product because parts may be difficult to obtain, the styles may change, or maybe the manufacturer no longer supports the model. There is a limited amount of time left before the item fails and gets thrown away or salvaged for scrap.

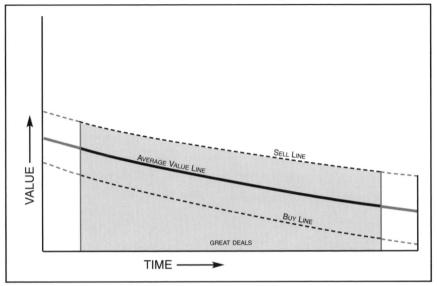

Figure 2.2 Great Deals Phase

GREAT DEALS IN MORE DETAIL

Let's take a look at the "Great Deals" phase in more detail as shown in Figure 2.2. An important concept to successfully buying preowned merchandise is to know when to buy and when to sell.

The beginning of this phase occurs after the greatest rate of depreciation, and the end is before costly repairs begin. Within this time period there is a lot of opportunity to buy at a low cost, use the item for a while, then sell it and buy an upgraded model.

Notice an upper and lower dashed line, which are called the Buy Line and the Sell Line. These lines represent the maximum and minimum values of the item at any given point. Since very few preowned items have a set value, there is always a range of what people believe it is worth. Most people will advertise an item for a price near the Sell Line. Of course as a consumer, the idea is to pay a price near the Buy Line. The key to being successful in the used market is to always purchase at or below the Buy Line. Anytime this occurs, you are getting a deal.

Once the item is bought at a bargain price, it can be used and enjoyed. After a period of time, advertise it for a price above or near the Sell Line. Since you paid a bargain price you can recoup up to 100% or more of your initial investment. This is basically free use during the time you have owned it. What a Great Deal!

TIME TO UPGRADE
Learning to recognize where you are on the Product Life Cycle can help you recoup your investment. Avoid getting caught in the downward spiral of repairs.

You may not even realize you are already following this principle. As products you own deteriorate, you replace them. Manufacturers count on this in order to keep a constant demand for their product. It is called planned obsolescence and products are designed with replacement in mind. But by following the Product Life Cycle principle, you can save yourself money in the process.

Now you can begin to see the potential profits. The buy and sell process requires little effort and the cost savings will more than make up for any inconvenience. The Product Life Cycle will vary in length depending on the product type, but in many cases the time between buying and selling can be years.

A CLEAN PROFIT

Let's look at an example of an everyday household appliance. Those of us who have made countless trips to the Laundromat value the convenience of owning a washing machine at home. When I decided to purchase an apartment size washer, I found the price tag on a new machine to be around $500.

As an alternative to buying new, I looked in the classified section and found several ads advertising the apartment size style. After just a few phone calls, I found a two year old washing machine used only a few times. Since the owner had bought a new house, he was storing this one in the garage still in the original box. His asking price was $275.

Since the washer was in immaculate condition, I offered $150. After a little negotiating, the owner settled on $200. Four years later when I moved, I sold the washer for $250, a $50 profit.

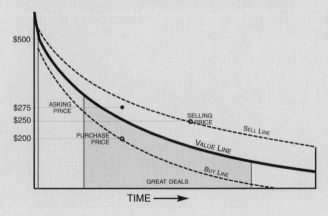

Getting Prepared

50% HUMOR

It's funny half the time!

FOR SALE: 20ft Motorboat in good running condition, slight damage. Must have scuba gear to see.

LOST: Husband and dog in the downtown area near the park, $100 reward for the dog.

FOR SALE: Four post bed, 115 years old. Perfect for antique lover.

TAKE THIS JOB AND $%&!!...Office equipment for sale. Desks, chairs, computers, best offer.

DESPERATE HOMEOWNER: Will trade 1 year old air conditioner for a working furnace.

CHAPTER

Buying preowned merchandise takes no more effort than buying the same item new. In fact, most people find that the process makes them a better consumer of both preowned and new items. The principles outlined here will help make you a more knowledgeable consumer and ensure your success.

It's so simple to begin. Start by creating a Wish List. What items do you want in your life? Which items do you need to replace? List the things you want to upgrade like a dining room set, patio

WISH LIST
Setting goals and priorities are an important part of the planning process. Writing them down will help you stay focused.

furniture or yard equipment, as well as items of enjoyment like a hot tub or big screen television. Don't restrict yourself or worry about how to acquire these items. For now just list all of your desires.

Once this list is complete, prioritize it. Which items are most important? Try to mix up your needs and desires because all work and no play can make for a stressful life. Include the whole family in creating a Wish List. Planning should be a fun and adventurous process.

WISH LIST

PRIORITY   I WISH I HAD / I NEED TO REPLACE...

_____   _____

_____   _____

_____   _____

_____   _____

_____   _____

_____   _____

_____   _____

_____   _____

_____   _____

_____   _____

_____   _____

_____   _____

_____   _____

_____   _____

_____   _____

_____   _____

_____   _____

Figure 3.1 Wish List: Use this form supplied in Appendix B to prioritize the items you need.

Take your list and put it somewhere visible so you can read it daily. For example, put it on the refrigerator so when you reach for a snack your list is there to review. It should be used as motivation towards achieving your goals. With each review you are securing a pattern for success in your subconscience. Eventually you will begin working toward financial success on a daily basis.

THINGS CHANGE
It is important to review your list periodically as your priorities may change.

Keeping your list in mind, let's review what could prevent you from accomplishing these goals. There are a couple of stumbling blocks everyone must overcome in order to succeed.

FEAR

Fear is a powerful emotion. Although it can have a positive effect in motivating you to fulfill your dreams, many people will let it deter them from taking action and getting started.

One of the most common reasons people do not get started buying preowned merchandise is their fear of failure. This fear can come from not knowing enough about an item, feeling inexperienced in spotting a deal or lacking the confidence to make an offer and negotiate on the price. If any of these reasons sound familiar to you, do not worry. With the simple techniques described in later chapters, you can overcome these fears and start on the road to success.

If you've had a bad experience in the past, do not let it deter you from trying again. Learning from experience is how we shape our lives. Rarely do you make the same mistake twice and next time you will have the techniques needed to succeed. Failure in the past does not determine your fate in the future.

WHY AM I SCARED TO START?
Acknowledge to yourself what might be preventing you from getting started and address those issues. As you become more knowledgeable, those fears will be replaced with confidence and a sense of accomplishment.

Take a look at successful people around you. One thing they have in common is that fear does not stand in their way. They use it as motivation to gain knowledge and aim for success. You can do the same.

If you have never shopped in the used market before, start with something small on your Wish List. Give it a try and build your confidence. You'll see how easy it is to begin.

CHANGE

Accepting change is a difficult task for many of us. We are all creatures of habit and this includes the way we purchase. Most of us have been conditioned through years of advertising to buy new expensive items even if we cannot afford them. Unfortunately this process has put many people into major financial troubles.

In addition, some people have been taught that buying preowned merchandise can be troublesome. Just say the phrase "used car" and many people automatically think headache even when they have never owned one. These responses are the result of influence

RECONDITIONING YOUR MIND
Start conditioning your mind and habits from one of spending money to one of saving money and you can experience a better quality of life.

from family, friends and advertisers. Unfortunately, it is these influences that prevent people from success. However, you can change that.

By simply changing your mind set you can change your purchasing habits and your response to such phrases. The used market can offer items that are practically new at extremely discounted prices. Making the change to buying in the used market can save you money and allow you to experience a greater value for your dollar. Eventually, when you hear the term "used car" you will think of "50% Off!"

EDUCATION

With your list in hand and your mind set for success, you can now begin to look, but not at preowned merchandise just yet. You first need to know how to identify a bargain.

When purchasing new products, most people compare various brands, models and store prices. The same should be true for buying preowned products. Your knowledge of the new market will give you a better insight into recognizing bargains in the used market.

CONSUMER REPORTS
Consumer Reports is a great tool for researching an item's quality or repair history. They give independent test results and accept no advertising. Consumer Reports will usually note the same problems you would find after owning the item.

Go to your local stores and talk with the salesmen about the different brands and models that work best. Many times what you find are small differences. The manufacturer may simply have added new colors or changed a few options.

PRICING GUIDES

Pricing Guides are a great way to know if you are getting a deal. Before going to look at an item for sale, check at least two pricing guides to determine the fair market value.

Above all, ask a lot of questions. Amazingly, the more questions you ask, the more answers you will get. While some answers will have little value, others may supply critical information. Analyze all the answers carefully. The salesperson is only trying to sell their product, but tap into their knowledge anyway. They may know basic information about the manufacturer, the ability to service the product promptly and the price differences for various options.

Go one step further and ask the local service center about the common repair problems they incur on the product. Based on the item's design or use, you may find certain models have more problems than others do.

Look at the quality of the products on the market. You may find that two major brands use the same major parts or are produced by the same manufacturer. The only difference besides the brand name may be the price. This is a common practice in many industries. If you believe this to be the case, be sure to check the repair track records as well.

SAME MANUFACTURER, DIFFERENT BRAND NAME

It is common in many industries that different name brand products are manufactured by the same company. Check with your local service center about brand name differences.

PLANNING

You are now ready to begin shopping in the used market, but be patient. Preowned products are constantly for sale, so there is no hurry to buy the first item you see.

Buy effectively by planning ahead. Try not to wait until your desire or need for the item is urgent, otherwise you could end up paying more than the item is worth.

THE SECRET'S IN THE PLANNING
Plan ahead to replace items before they deteriorate and fail.

Since market demand generally determines price, sometimes buying off season can save you money. For example, a seller advertising a motorboat would probably get a higher price in the spring than in the late fall. But commonly, people advertise them in the fall to avoid storing these boats for the winter. Since the demand for boats is usually less in the fall than the spring, you would probably find a better price.

When it comes to upgrading a product you have now, do not wait until it is about to break down. You will only lose on the resale value and may not have the option of bargaining on the one you need to buy. The fact is most items deteriorate slowly over time showing signs of wear along the way. Poor planning will cost you every time, but planning ahead can yield significant results.

Where to Look

50% HUMOR

It's funny half the time!

FOR SALE: 1 man/3 woman hot tub, $650, wife says it must go.

ANNOYED PARENT: Will trade 12 month old Cockatiel for a less noisy animal.

FOR SALE: Queen size sofa bed, good condition, $250, tired of visitors.

FOR SALE: Computer, 17" monitor, 3GHD, modem, color printer, looks great on a desk even if you don't know how to operate it.

FREE: Firewood, no longer need, house burned down.

CHAPTER

How do you find great deals? The ways are as endless as your imagination. Goods and services can be found at reduced prices everywhere from the general classified ads to the Internet. Let's look at the different places to locate these bargains.

LOCAL NEWSPAPER CLASSIFIED ADS

Local newspapers are the most common and usually the first place to look for everyday items for sale. It is generally local people advertising items they want to sell quickly. Most papers categorize the ads into specific headings such as automobiles, general merchandise, garden and yard tools, boats, wanted to buy and so on. Each paper has a method of listing ads under a category. For example, take the automobile category. Some papers will list by year, make or model while others may list in chronological order. Once you

> **WHERE ARE THE NEW ADS?**
> Call your local newspaper to find out where new ads are placed. Some papers place them at the beginning of the section while others place them alphabetically. This way you can quickly locate the new ads and be the first to call.

become familiar with each newspaper, you can scan the ads quickly to find what you are looking to buy.

> **ORIGINAL OWNER**
> The best buying opportunities usually come from private individuals who bought the item new.

There are all different kinds of classified newspapers. Some specialize in nothing but paid advertising for both commercial and private individuals. Some smaller local papers may offer free ads to local patrons, subsidized with commercial advertising in between. None the less, all of these publications are great sources for finding items you need.

Be careful of answering ads placed by commercial dealers who use the local classified ads to advertise their products. Your chances of obtaining a deal from them are slim. They are professional sellers who usually have to account for overhead costs. The best opportunities will come from private individuals or homeowners.

NATIONAL CLASSIFIED ADS

There are publications that contain classified ads nationwide. Many of these publications list items that need a larger exposure such as antique cars or other collectibles, but there are some that advertise a broader range of merchandise.

Generally, these ads offer little buying opportunity for general merchandise. Many times the item is too far away to view or the shipping costs take away from your savings. In these cases, national publications are best used in helping you obtain an idea of the item's worth before buying or selling.

WANTED TO BUY CLASSIFIED ADS

Are you looking for a particular item but just can't seem to find it for sale? Try placing an ad in the "Wanted to Buy" section of your local newspaper. When the item you want does not appear

> **A WINNING AD**
> When writing "Wanted to Buy" ads, be cautious of the wording. Many people mistake them as "For Sale" ads. Try including the terms "Wanted to buy" or "In search of" in your ad.

for sale very often or is not easily found, advertise your search so others will know you are interested. Someone out there may have exactly what you want and be willing to sell it, but just doesn't have the initiative to advertise. Your ad may spark their interest to give you a call.

INTERNET CLASSIFIED ADS

With computers becoming standard equipment in the home and office, the Internet is now one of the quickest places to find information. Many local newspapers and national publications have created web sites offering news, sports and free classified ads.

The Internet is excellent for scanning publications quickly. Many classified ad sections are maintained in a database so you can search by location, description or other parameters, zooming in quickly on the items you need. Within just a

> **CATCH THE LATEST UPDATE**
> Find out when the Internet site updates the classified section. Then try to read these ads right after the updates so you can be the first to respond.

few minutes you can scan all the statewide classified ads in a fraction of the time it would take to read the newspapers.

INTERNET AUCTIONS

This has quickly become a hot item on the Internet with the concept being very similar to a regular auction house. People who have items for sale

TOUCH OF A BUTTON
Take advantage of the information super highway. Online auctions, local newspaper web sites, and online classifieds offer an array of preowned items. The Internet can save you valuable time and money.

place an advertisement on an auction house web site for a set number of days. Interested parties bid on the items and when the auction expires, the highest bid wins. This is a great way to sell your items and attract a large number of potential buyers quickly.

However, when buying through an online auction, be careful. Make sure that the item you are considering comes from a reputable source. Many of the online auctions offer reviews sent in by previous customers. Be sure to read these, but realize that anyone can submit them, even the seller.

BULLETIN BOARDS

Bulletin boards are also a great place to find items for sale. Many grocery stores, local retailers and libraries will have an area where customers can place an advertisement for no cost. Some people put their business cards up hoping to generate business while others list household items for sale.

It is advantageous to review these bulletin boards occasionally because the likelihood for competition to buy is minimal. The merchandise for sale is generally local as well, so time can be saved in traveling.

RADIO STATIONS

There are even local radio stations that dedicate weekly programs to selling preowned items. The radio stations let the listeners call in and talk about the items for sale. Then people who are interested can call in and ask questions. It makes buying and selling entertaining and fun. Check with your local radio station to see if they offer such programming.

BACKYARDS

This is an all time favorite place to look for items. Bargains are everywhere. As you travel around town, look for items you are interested in purchasing. If it appears that the owner may only be storing it, stop and

> **LET'S MAKE A DEAL**
> Locating items before they are advertised can eliminate the competition and offer some great deals.

inquire with the owner. More times than not, the owner is receptive to the idea of selling. He just may lack the initiative or knowledge to advertise the item for sale. You can offer what the item is worth to you and if the seller agrees or negotiates on the price, you can close the deal.

WORD OF MOUTH

Make sure you let your family, friends, neighbors and coworkers know what you are looking to purchase. They may know of someone who wants to sell such an item. It is that simple and it works! Think of this as a verbal classified ad.

Networking and communicating with other people are excellent methods to let others know of your intentions to purchase or sell. There are many businesses that rely on this principle to generate sales. You can use the same idea to find items with little effort. The more eyes helping you look, the quicker you can achieve success.

VERBAL CLASSIFIED ADS
Some of the best deals you may find will result from word of mouth. It seems someone is always storing the item you need and just hasn't advertised it yet.

Telephone
Conversations

50% HUMOR

It's funny half the time!

FOR SALE: 14HP Tractor, 36" cut, $650. Must sell, wife says I need exercise.

FOR SALE: Two dairy cows, never bred. Also one gay bull, best offer.

WILL TRADE: 14 ft. Rowboat with small hole, for something that floats.

FOR SALE: Toaster, $15, automatically burns toast.

FOR SALE: 1970's and 80's Art deco furnishings. Got married, can no longer keep, best offers.

CHAPTER

Once you find the desired items for sale, it's time to call for more information. Since this is the initial contact with the seller, there are several things you should be aware of when discussing an item on the telephone.

DEVELOP RAPPORT

The initial goal of any conversation is to develop rapport so the seller will share detailed information about an item. Introduce yourself and volunteer your first name. Then ask what the seller's name is and include it in your conversation. Your telephone conversation could go something like this:

> **Buyer:** "Hello, My name is Joe. I am calling about the Jacuzzi you advertised in the local newspaper. May I ask who I am talking to?"
>
> **Seller:** "My name is Tom."
>
> **Buyer:** "Hi Tom, what can you tell me about the Jacuzzi you have for sale?"

Something as simple as the exchange of first names can break down the barriers between two strangers. People are more willing to share information and negotiate with friends or friendly people, so be polite. Developing that initial trust with the seller can make him feel comfortable in conversing with you and sharing the details of the item.

SUM UP THE ITEM QUALITY

You should develop a list of questions to ask the seller before you call. Here are some sample questions to get you started:

- Are you the original owner?
- How long have you owned the item?
- Where was it purchased?
- Why are you selling the item?
- Is your price negotiable?
- What color is it?
- How frequently was the item used?
- How many miles or hours has the item accumulated?
- What is the condition of the item?
- Are there any service records? Who serviced the item? (service center or owner)
- How often was it serviced?
- Have any parts been replaced? If so, when?
- Are there any dents, nicks, scratches, tears, etc.?
- Is there any damage or has any damage been repaired?
- What is your best price?

Work your questions into the conversation to create a discussion about the item and its use. To keep the conversation flowing, let the seller's answers guide you into asking more detailed questions. Be sure to maintain a very positive and friendly attitude. By the end of the conversation, you should have a clear picture as to the product's condition, price and features.

> **?? QUESTIONS ??**
> It is important to get as much information as possible over the telephone. Write down your questions ahead of time so you won't forget to ask.

In Appendix B of this book you will find the Buyer Worksheet (Figure 5.1). This worksheet was designed to assist you in compiling information about the item for sale. Recording important information will minimize any confusion if you are calling several advertisements.

Make copies of the worksheet and keep them handy when calling on advertisements. As you talk with the seller, write down the details of the item on the Buyer Worksheet. If you do not go see the item immediately, the worksheet will provide valuable information in the future.

NEGOTIATE OVER THE TELEPHONE

Before venturing out to look at an item you should try to determine the seller's flexibility. If the item is in good condition and the price is acceptable or negotiable, it may be worth a trip to view it. If the item is in poor condition, overpriced or the seller insists he is firm, do not waste your time. There is no point in looking at an overpriced item when a seller refuses to negotiate.

BUYER WORKSHEET

DATE _____ FOUND AD IN _____

SELLER'S NAME _____ ADDRESS _____

TELEPHONE NO. _____

PRODUCT MAKE/MODEL _____ YEAR/AGE _____

ASKING PRICE _____ BEST PRICE _____ ☐ NEGOTIABLE

OTHER _____

CONDITION/USE _____

REPAIRS/REPLACEMENT PARTS _____

DIRECTIONS _____

Figure 5.1 Buyer Worksheet: Use the Buyer Worksheet in Appendix B to record valuable information when responding to advertisements.

Many sellers inflate the asking price so there is room to negotiate while others may price an item at the fair market value. For this reason, make a point to ask these questions in your conversation:

· Is your price negotiable?
· What is your best price?

If you look at the list of questions provided earlier in this chapter, you will notice that these questions are not listed together. Although both questions are similar, they sometimes yield very different results. Ask them at different times in the conversation and you may be surprised by the answers.

Determining the
Seller's Motivation

50% HUMOR

It's funny half the time!

FOR SALE: Parachute, like new. Only used once, never opened, $500.

SWF, loyal, trustworthy good looking girl with blonde hair and dark eyes seeks companionship. Loves long walks in the woods, hunting, camping, fishing trips and cozy winter nights by the fireplace. I'll meet you at the front door with a kiss when you get home from a hard day at work. Call the animal shelter and ask for Goldie.

FOR SALE: Mobile home, 3BR, 1 BTH, double wide, scenic views (Depending on where you park it).

TIRED OF FINDING PARKING: Will trade, stretch limo in excellent condition in exchange for a shorter vehicle.

FOR SALE: One person rope hammock, must sell. "Honey do list" is getting long, $75.

CHAPTER

To bargain effectively it is essential to understand the seller's personality and motivation. With a few good questions you can quickly evaluate any situation.

Some people may never share their reasons for selling while others may reveal their life stories. Most sellers are just average people adjusting to life's changes. Their families grow or situations change that cause them to sell off items that are no longer needed.

It is time to play detective and uncover as much information as possible. Let's review some of the main reasons people sell.

SPRING CLEANING

It never fails. When the weather turns warm, people decide to clean out the clutter in the attic, basement or garage. Soon the classified ads are filled with unwanted items, many of which are still in great condition. As a buyer, this can be an ideal situation.

> **GETTING IN SHAPE**
>
> How many rowing machines or exercise bikes have you seen that have worn out from use? The next time you see an infomercial for exercise equipment you want, don't pick up the telephone and order it. Instead, look through the classified ad section of your local newspaper. Most likely you can find the same item at a much better price.

In most cases the seller's goal is to just move the item out of the house. Many times he doesn't remember the original price or know what the fair market value is. If the only option is to store it for another year, the price may be negotiable.

MONEY PROBLEMS

In today's society, credit is easily available. Banks, stores and mortgage companies make it very easy to create debt. Advertisements reading "Buy Now, Pay Later" attract people who desire instant gratification, but can't afford the purchase.

Sadly, many people lack the money management skills to stay out of debt. It is all too common that people overextend themselves and have no way to get out of financial distress. Simply put, many sellers need money.

> **OVEREXTENDED**
>
> The monetary distress scenario is common among couples who buy based on two incomes. When one of them is suddenly out of work or stays home to raise a child, they start selling off assets to generate cash flow and reduce debt.

So how do you know if you have this situation? During your conversation be sure to ask, "Why are you selling?" Sometimes the response is as simple as, "I just can't afford to keep it." You may find that the seller begins telling you about his financial situation. Pay close attention. The responses could give you the clues to monetary distress.

While viewing the item, observe the surroundings. Take notice of the new car or boat, new home, or nice setting. Nothing is wrong with a nice lifestyle, but if the income or job doesn't match the lifestyle, you may have a financial distress situation.

REPLACEMENT

A common reason for selling is to replace an older item with a newer model. Many people just like the idea of owning brand new items and sell the older ones after very little use. Once an owner has decided to replace an item, there is a need to

> **REPLACEMENT COSTS**
> The replacement scenario can offer a great purchasing opportunity, but only if the item is still in good condition. Avoid those sellers who are selling the item too late in the Product Life Cycle.

sell the older one. Either he needs to make room for the new model, or he might need the money for a down payment.

The easiest way to determine this situation is to ask a few questions such as, "Why are you selling" or "Did you buy a new one?" Most owners are proud to talk about their new purchases. Many times they will reveal some of the problems they had with the item for sale while discussing the newer model they just purchased.

ENVIRONMENTAL CHANGES

Our lives are constantly changing. Moving to a new home, new career, a newborn child, illness, divorce, death or even winning the lottery are just some of the many changes people go through in life. All of these changes cause us to reevaluate the need for items we own.

Many of these items appearing on the market from this scenario are in excellent condition. Since the owner needs to make room for life's changes, price may be negotiable.

When negotiating on an item being sold, be aware of the seller's emotions. In the case of a new career, newborn child or winning the lottery, a seller will be very excited about the change so selling the item may be very easy.

However, in cases of distress like divorce or death, you may encounter resentment and anger. Realize that the sale of these items can be difficult for the seller so lending a sympathetic ear may ease the transaction.

EMOTIONAL ATTACHMENT

A seller can be emotionally attached to an item that is being sold. He may be selling something that was in the family for generations or represents meaningful memories.

These emotional bonds can result in the owner pricing an item at a higher value than it is worth and insisting that the price is not negotiable. When you present an offer in this type of situation, an owner's response may be, "For that price I might as well keep it." Here are some suggestions on how to diffuse such a situation.

TIPS TO DIFFUSE EMOTIONAL ATTACHMENT
  ✓ Be an empathetic listener
  ✓ Explain that the item has a fair market value

First, recognize the situation and be an empathetic listener. Encourage the owner to reminisce about the memories. He may come to realize that the memories do not warrant the price and separate the emotions from the material item. After all, the conscious decision to sell it has already been made.

Secondly, explain tactfully that the item has a certain fair market value, but be careful not to insult the owner. He may be proud of the item or cherish the memories so being intolerant of his feelings could cause him to get angry. With a calming, empathetic approach, it is possible to achieve a win/win negotiation.

If for some reason you could not negotiate a reasonable agreement, allow some time. The owner may just need more time to reassess the sale and come to terms with the value

TIME TO THINK
Situations are always changing. If an owner is not negotiable, save the telephone number and call back after a short period of time.

of the item. Save the telephone number and call back after a short period of time to see if he has reconsidered.

RECOGNIZING THE DISHONEST SELLER

Be aware! There are sellers who may not disclose truthful information on the item for sale. Although the majority of people are honest, some may simply distort the truth about its condition.

It is your money at risk so be aware of situations that may raise warning flags. These could include:

- The seller offers nothing but rave reviews on the item.
- The seller refuses to discuss the price until you look at the item.
- The information may be inconsistent throughout the conversation.
- The seller makes you feel uncomfortable with the situation.
- The seller may tell you he is watching out for your best interests.
- The seller insists on meeting you somewhere other than his home or business.
- If it is too good to be true, it probably is.

Do not deal with people whose character you find questionable. If you have the impression you

VERIFY THE OWNER
To avoid being a victim of purchasing stolen items, check titles or receipts against the actual item when possible.

are dealing with a dishonest seller, walk away. There is always another deal waiting for you.

Quickly assessing the seller's situation can aid in your negotiations. But above all, use your common sense and good judgment to enjoy the many opportunities in the used market.

Closing

the Deal

50% HUMOR

It's funny half the time!

FOR SALE: 12HP Snow blower, used only on snowy days, $150.

FOR SALE: Exercise bike, hardly used, $300, call Chubbie.

LOST: Small white poodle, reward, neutered, like one of the family.

FOR SALE: Recliner chair, blue, contemporary style, custom built beer holder, $200.

ANNOYED MECHANIC'S WIFE WILL TRADE: Old Mustang GT Convertible for a vehicle that runs.

CHAPTER

When negotiating and closing the deal, it's time to bring together all of your knowledge and skills. The techniques described in this chapter can help you keep control of the situation and achieve a successful transaction.

THINGS TO BRING WITH YOU

Some basic tools can make viewing an item less time consuming and reduce the risk of overlooking important information. Bring along a flashlight in case the item is in a poorly lit area or you plan to view the item at night. A screwdriver and pliers can be helpful if you need to open a cover or make a minor adjustment. If you plan on taking the item home in your car, you may need rope and a pocketknife. You may not use all these items, but having them at your disposal prepares you

THINGS TO BRING WITH YOU
- ✓ Flashlight
- ✓ Screwdriver
- ✓ Pliers
- ✓ Rope
- ✓ Pocketknife
- ✓ Bill of Sale
- ✓ Money

for almost any circumstance you encounter. Much like any good Boy Scout knows, "always be prepared!"

FIRST IMPRESSIONS

First impressions play a dramatic role in day to day life and the used market is no different. The seller will form an impression as you get out of your car, walk up the driveway and introduce yourself. Your car, clothing, body language and general demeanor will set the stage for the initial conversations. So exhibit a confident posture, offer a firm handshake and state a friendly "Hello." After all, first impressions are lasting.

Since your appearance will have an impression on the seller, it should be used to your advantage. Showing up in your Sunday best driving a new BMW may make it appear as if you have money to spend. The understated approach is usually more successful. Wearing casual clothes like a T-shirt and jeans would be more appropriate. Drive the everyday car to give the impression that you are an average person of a moderate income. After all, you are shopping for a deal.

BREAKING THE ICE
Complimenting the seller on something you see in their home or yard is a great way to break the tension and start a conversation.

How you act can affect the negotiating process so retain your composure and avoid getting emotional. If you exhibit a lot of anxiety about buying an item, the seller may hold firm on the price. Remain confident and appear knowledgeable. If you have done your homework before shopping, you should have no trouble conversing intelligently and knowledgeably about the item. Remember that your entire behavior contributes to the first impression.

Most of all, be careful not to intimidate the seller. Never exhibit arrogance or you will certainly offend him and lose a good buying opportunity. Your goal should be to create a comfortable exchange of information.

A little humor can help break down any tensions, but be cautious about telling any bad jokes. Sometimes a joke that you think is funny may offend other people. Use your best judgment and take note of the seller's reactions. Many times these reactions can speak louder than words.

> **HELPFUL HINTS**
> How the seller maintains the house, yard or other surroundings can be a good indication of the item's condition and maintenance.

Just as the seller is assessing you, you should be taking note of a few things as well. As you approach the house or are invited inside, take note of the surroundings. If the house or yard is nicely maintained, you may assume the owner takes care of his possessions. These simple clues can provide information as to the item's quality and maintenance.

ASK QUESTIONS

Be sure to ask a lot of questions. The seller's response, hesitation or avoidance to your questions can tell you a lot about an item he is selling. As you look over the item you need to develop more specific questions on its condition, how it was used, repairs, problems, parts, service, warranties, etc. Some basic questions were provided in Chapter Five to get you started.

> **SECOND OPINION**
> When going to look at an item for sale, consider going
> with a friend. While you analyze the condition of the
> item and talk with the seller, your friend can converse
> with someone else to see if any information conflicts. If
> only the seller is present, at least you have two people
> asking questions to determine the condition.

Pay careful attention to the answers. This is your chance to
reveal the dishonest seller. Rephrase your questions and ask
them at different stages of the conversation. If the responses are
inconsistent, you may have uncovered a problem.

Take this opportunity to look it all over, try it out, test all the
knobs, buttons and levers, give it a test run, and be thoroughly
convinced that everything works to your satisfaction. If you have
any doubt, make that known to the seller and use it to negotiate
the price down. Inform him that you are willing to take a chance
on buying it, but will need some money to get the item repaired.

WALK AWAY

Being able to walk away from an item for sale is a powerful
negotiating tool. Always remember that it's your money you are
spending, so there is no pressure to buy.

Before you go out looking at an item for sale, you should have a
maximum price in mind. Try not to go over this limit. If you
reach this limit during the negotiating, simply stop increasing
your offer. Too many times a buyer will fall in love with the
color, style or new condition, but this is no reason to overpay. If
it's not a deal, then you are not interested.

If you can't reach an agreeable price with the seller, thank him for his time, wish him luck in selling

> **DO NOT GO OVER YOUR LIMIT**
> Before you go out to look at an item for sale, you should have a maximum price in mind.

the item and walk way. Leave your name and telephone number and remind the seller to call you if he changes his mind. This can be a great bargaining tool when used properly.

After a brief period of time has lapsed, telephone the seller back and remake your offer. If the seller still does not want to negotiate on the price, save the telephone number for future consideration.

> **IT'S IN THE DEAL**
> Great deals are made when buying. You have the money and the ability to negotiate. Buy at a low price and you should have no trouble recovering your investment.

Many times sellers will try to pressure you into buying by stating, "I have someone else coming to look." Although this may be true in some cases, many times it is only used to pressure you into the sale. Avoid impulse buying just because the seller pressures you. Remember that you are in control and can walk away. Most likely you can find another one advertised at a much more reasonable price.

Upon occasion the seller may question you about his asking price or the item's condition. "Not a bad price for its condition, don't you think?" Be careful how you respond as the seller is looking to validate his asking price.

To deflect such a comment, respond with a question of your own, "Why did you say you are selling it?" or be up front with a reply such as, "I expected the condition to be better for the price." Either method can be very effective.

MAKING THE OFFER

Remember that the goal is to purchase the item at or below its fair market value. This way when you resell it, you can make a profit or at least break even. Having done your homework, you should know what the item is really worth and how much of a market demand there is. From talking with the seller, you should also have an idea of the owner's reasons for selling and how anxious he is to sell.

Once you have decided what the item is worth to you, you should have some idea where you want to start your bidding. It is always best to make the initial offer before any discussion on the price takes place. If the seller names the first figure, the starting price may be too high along with his expectations.

> **MAKE AN OFFER**
> Always make the initial offer. If the seller names the first figure, the starting price may be too high.

Try to bring the bidding to a close quickly. The longer the bidding goes on, the more you could pay. If the seller will not lower the price, remind him you can pay in cash now. Don't worry if the conversation goes silent during bidding, the seller is probably thinking seriously about your offer. Avoid trying to make idle conversation, let the silence remain. After all, this can be a big decision for him.

If your accepted offer was below the market price, it doesn't mean the seller is disappointed. He may be pleased to know the item is going to someone who can really use it. Or it's very possible your low offer is more than the seller expected to get in the beginning. The seller may just be happy to have the item out of the garage or basement, and taking possession of the item at the time of sale may be enough to make the seller content. There are many reasons the seller could be satisfied, but having done your homework, you can make the seller's motivation work for you. This can be a win/win situation.

MAKING PAYMENT

There are many methods in which you can pay the seller but in the used market, "Cash is King!" Many sellers are willing to take a lower price for the item if it means instant cash. It's common to hear a seller say, "the first one with cash takes it."

But this doesn't mean overlooking the option of paying by personal check. If you can convince the seller to accept a check it may be to your advantage. A personal check can give you time to cancel payment if what you bought was misrepresented or had a problem that you were not told about.

But the seller might have similar concerns that you could cancel payment or do not have sufficient funds in your account. Unless you have developed a trusting relationship with the seller, cash will be the payment of choice.

In some circumstances of larger valued items, a seller may take a deposit and hold an item until you can return with the remainder of the money. Be sure to get a receipt stating the deposit, the amount owed and the terms of your agreement. However, be prepared to forfeit your deposit if you do not hold up to your part of the

> ### MAKING CHANGE
> Keep a portion of your cash in small bills so you have room to negotiate. It is difficult to offer $80 and ask for change from a $100 bill. Plan ahead.

BILL OF SALE
(GENERAL)

SELLER (OWNER)	NAME	
	ADDRESS	
	CITY, STATE, ZIP	
PURCHASER	NAME	
	ADDRESS	
	CITY, STATE, ZIP	
SELLING PRICE	$	The owner of the item described below hereby transfers ownership to the purchaser in consideration of the selling price.
DESCRIPTION		
SIGNATURE	I declare that the information provided above is true to the best of my knowledge and belief.	
	SIGNATURE OF SELLER	DATE

Figure 7.1 Bill of Sale (General): The Bill of Sale forms in Appendix B can be used to record your purchase.

agreement. It is possible the seller might sell the item to someone else at a lesser price with your deposit making up the difference.

However you decide to pay for a purchase, it's always important to obtain a Bill of Sale or a receipt. This is your proof that you paid for an item and took ownership. The Bill of Sale should state all the conditions of the item: make, model, serial number, etc. It should state the deposit amount, the balance due and method of payment (i.e. cash, personal check, bank check). It could also include any terms regarding delivery or how long you have to pick up the item. Make sure it is signed and dated by both parties. Appendix B provides some sample Bill of Sale forms.

Many sellers will want the phrase "as is" written on the Bill of Sale. Basically it means that you, the buyer, accept the condition of the item at the time of sale. It is used to protect the seller in case after the purchase you discover a problem and want to return it. So if you buy an item "as is", be sure you have looked it over thoroughly and are satisfied with the condition.

A CHECKLIST FOR CLOSING THE DEAL:
- ✓ Check the VIN (Vehicle Identification Number) on the title against the item (if applicable).
- ✓ Make sure the person selling the item is the owner or has the authority to sell the item. If uncertain, ask the person for ID to verify against the title.
- ✓ Obtain a Bill of Sale listing the specifics of the sale (i.e. seller/buyer names, item description, deposit, balance due, serial number, date, etc.)

The Bill of Sale forms provided in the Appendix do not contain the clause "as is", but if the seller insists and you feel comfortable, you may need to write this phrase on your form.

If a title is involved for items such as a car, boat, etc., make sure all the appropriate paperwork is properly signed and dated. It's important to verify all identification numbers on the paperwork with the numbers on the item. Even owners with the best of intentions sometimes confuse information.

HONOR

Occasionally you may meet someone who insists on doing business like in the old days, "with a handshake." It is a pleasure to meet these people who take pride in their promises. But unfortunately in today's world, use this approach as a last resort if you are serious about a purchase. Without a written agreement, there is no assurance that an owner will hold an item until you return with payment or take possession.

Turning Items
into Cash

50% HUMOR

It's funny half the time!

DUSTY

One couple we know has stored their exercise bike for so long the family named it "Dusty." Ironically, instead of using it for exercise, it was put on rollers so they could push it out of the way. Needless to say it will soon be advertised for sale stating "low mileage."

THE REAL USES FOR EXERCISE EQUIPMENT:

- ✓ Clothesline
- ✓ To fill the spare bedroom and discourage the kids from moving back home
- ✓ A shelf to hold the workout videos
- ✓ Door stop
- ✓ So you can tell others you have a gym
- ✓ A beer holder
- ✓ Boat Anchor
- ✓ To put the remote on while you watch Football

CHAPTER

With a few simple techniques you can sell your items quickly and easily. Knowing how to sell effectively can also help make you a more knowledgeable consumer and a better negotiator in the used market.

PRESENTATION

Before advertising an item for sale, take a few moments to clean it up and make it look presentable. Gather all the attachments, manuals and related equipment so the item is complete when someone comes to look. A few minutes of preparation can make for a better presentation and a quicker, more profitable sale.

After cleaning the item, consider the location where you will show it. Put the item somewhere accessible like the garage, porch or living room rather than leaving it in the attic or basement. You will want to place the item in

> **LOCATION, LOCATION, LOCATION!**
> It's not just for Real Estate. Always showcase your item where it will make the best impression on the buyer.

the best possible location to make it visually appealing. For example, a sofa bed would display a lot better in a living room than in a dusty garage setting.

If the item requires electrical or water hookup, make sure that these facilities are readily available. Most people will want to see an item work before they make the investment. A proper presentation can make the sale.

ESTABLISH THE SELL PRICE

Review the Product Life Cycle in Chapter Two and get a general idea of what stage your item is in. Be realistic about the item's condition and value because if your price is too high, buyers may quickly lose interest.

If you're unsure of the value, visit your local retail store to see the cost of the newer models. This will give you an idea of the competition with your item. Then review and call a few ads in the classified section to determine the asking price of similar items.

Once you have determined the true value of the item, you need to determine the asking price. There are a few things to remember. First, your goal is to break even with the price you originally paid. Doing so will mean you used the item for no cost during the time you have owned it. A great savings!

SAVING DEPRECIATION
Selling durable goods at the same price you paid means you have avoided depreciation and had free use of the item. Repeatedly doing this can add up to tremendous savings.

But you must be realistic and ask yourself if the condition would warrant that price. If you maintained the item and are selling it within the "Great Deal" phase of the Product Life Cycle, then you can most likely recover your investment.

A second point to consider is that people like to feel they are getting a deal. That means buyers expect to negotiate on price and doing so can make the buyer feel satisfied, a win/win situation. Knowing this, consider raising your asking price slightly so you have room to negotiate with the buyer.

EFFECTIVE ADVERTISING

A winning ad will encourage more people to call. Just listing the item itself may not be enough to get the responses you want. Include information that is helpful to the buyer such as the make, model, color, general condition, price and so on. Try to be creative with each piece of information, describing it in a positive tone. An effective advertisement is one of your best opportunities to generate calls.

EFFECTIVE ADVERTISING TERMS
Use positive words when describing an item for sale such as:

✓ Barely Used	✓ Cherry	✓ Excellent Condition
✓ Flawless	✓ Like New	✓ Low Hours
✓ Meticulous	✓ Mint	✓ Original Owner
✓ Perfect	✓ Spotless	✓ Under Warranty

Everything you learned in Chapter Four (Where to Look) now applies to advertising. Focus in on areas where you suspect there is going to be a demand for your item. Place the advertisement in areas where you have looked for items to buy yourself such as free bulletin boards or local classified ads.

Remember to consider the cost of advertising when calculating your profits on the resale. On higher priced items this may not be a concern, but on lower priced goods you might want to look for free places to advertise.

BE SAFE

Before giving directions to your home, attempt to get the buyer's name and telephone number. You may even want to ask him how many people are coming to look at the item. If he is curious why you are asking, just tell him you are trying to be safe. Most people will respect your honesty. If he refuses to give you this information, you may not want to continue with the directions.

SAFETY IN NUMBERS
Make sure someone else is home or with you when a potential buyer comes to visit.

When the buyer does come to your home to view items, keep him from wondering around. Avoid revealing personal information about you or your family. Although most people are honest, be aware of the few who might prey upon your kindness and hospitality.

SALES APPROACH

You don't need to be a salesperson to sell your item. Many times the buyer is in such a need that the item practically sells itself. However, there are a few things to think about during this selling process.

All the techniques you have learned in the previous chapters still apply even though you are on the other end of the sale. You should be prepared for a buyer just like yourself who is going to ask detailed questions and try to negotiate on price.

Remember all the techniques regarding telephone conversations. You should work on developing rapport with the buyer so any negotiations will go smoothly. Ask a first name and use it in your conversation. Much of the sale may actually take place on the telephone before the buyer comes to look at the item.

Chapter Seven discussed the techniques needed to close a deal. All of these apply when selling an item as well. Since first impressions count, be the average person just moving along an item. Present a good appearance and consider the path the buyer will take through your house. You may want to avoid passing through the messy garage to show the item for sale.

You should be prepared for a buyer who asks very detailed questions about the item. Remember to be honest in your answers and avoid rambling on. Answer the buyer's questions with brief concise responses.

When negotiations start, if the buyer didn't name the first price, you are in the driver's seat. You may want to slightly lower your price to show good faith, but name a price relatively higher than your bottom line. The buyer may be so happy that you came down, the negotiations would be over quickly.

THE BUYER WANTS A DEAL
Coming down slightly in price during negotiations can set the buyer at ease and close the deal quickly.

If necessary, offer incentives instead of reducing the price. For example, you might offer to store the item for a few days until the buyer can arrange for a way to pick it up. You may even offer to deliver it to his home, or assist in hooking it up.

As for making payment, remember, "Cash is King." Only accept cash or bank checks to avoid any problems of stopping payment or insufficient funds. If the buyer is sincere about the purchase, he will have no problem producing cash.

The selling process can be a lot of fun if you follow some of these simple rules. Remember that all the techniques you have learned to become an effective buyer are applicable in selling circumstances. Be honest with yourself and potential buyers and you will enjoy the many rewards of the used market.

No Money Deals

BLIND MAN WILL TRADE: 3BR, 1BTH, home overlooking nudist resort for house of equal value.

FOR SALE: Drill press, table saw, nail gun, must sell to pay for hospital bill, best offer.

MOTHER WILL TRADE: 4 ft Iguana with homemade tank in exchange for a smaller pet.

FOR SALE: Bathroom vanity, oak with brass handles, $150, it thinks it looks great.

EXERCISE EQUIPMENT FOR SALE: Queen size mattress and box spring, $175.

GOLF IS NOT MY SPORT: Will trade 15 Hours of golf lessons and new clubs for use of vacation home.

How about obtaining the items on your Wish List without using money? The used market can offer these and other opportunities through the power of bartering.

Bartering, also commonly referred to as trading, is simply the exchange of one commodity for another. Some people choose to trade durable goods while others choose to trade their services. In either case, there are many creative opportunities available to you.

SPECIFIC ADVERTISING

A specific barter advertisement lets the reader know the items or services available and which items or services would be accepted in trade.

> WILL TRADE: 1 yr. old 18HP tractor, excellent condition for waverunner of equal value

The advantage to writing specific advertisements is that only people who have the items you are looking to purchase will respond. If you are not willing to accept other items, then this can be an effective advertising method.

GENERAL ADVERTISING

If you're looking for a method to generate a lot of interest, then general advertising is the method to choose. A general advertisement simply lets the reader know about the item you have and encourages him to call with any ideas or items he might have to trade.

> WILL TRADE: 1 yr. old 18HP tractor, excellent condition in exchange for anything of equal value.

A classified ad like this can produce many calls with offers to trade practically anything. You can then choose which, if any, of the offers you would like.

In some cases you can trade for a higher valued item that you may then sell for a profit. With a general advertisement, the offers are only as limited as the imagination of people.

> **DECISIONS, DECISIONS**
> Use general advertisements and you may find people will call with a wide range of items to trade.

CASH DEALS

Many times you can buy items that are listed in the barter section. If you see an item of interest and you do not have something to trade, consider calling the seller and making an offer. Many people are more than willing to take cash for items they have. Since the seller has not set a predetermined price, you can offer what the item is worth to you.

BE CREATIVE

Bartering can be as creative as you allow it to be in both advertising and negotiating. Some of the most amazing deals you will ever hear about result from trading. Avoid limiting your ideas and read the barter section with a simple thought in mind, satisfy the seller's

> **WIN/WIN NEGOTIATING**
> Be a creative problem solver. Satisfy the seller's need and the deal will fall into place.

needs. As long as both parties involved are happy, you can trade most anything. Here are just a few examples of some creative barter advertisements.

WILL TRADE: 4 year Gym membership worth $2000 for anything of equal value.

WILL TRADE: Harley Davidson Sportster, full chrome, low miles for ski boat with trailer.

WILL TRADE: Season passes to water theme park for season baseball tickets.

IN SEARCH OF: Above ground swimming pool in exchange for children's jungle gym. The kids have grown.

WILL TRADE: Summer home in South Carolina for land in Florida.

WILL TRADE: Deer permits on private land for use of snowmobile trails in Maine.

WILL TRADE: Part of time share in Bermuda for part of time share in other areas.

How to Start
Today

50% HUMOR

It's funny half the time!

FREE TO GOOD HOME: 2 Black lab puppies, 7 weeks old, 555-1234, leave mess.

FOR SALE: Mixing bowl set designed to please a cook with round bottom.

BACHELOR WILL TRADE: Guitar lessons for house cleaning services.

FREE: 3BR, 2BTH home, good location with the purchase of a $152,000 welcome mat.

FOR SALE: Golf clubs, defective, always slice, $50.

GETTING MARRIED SALE: HIS: Neon beer signs, disco ball, 10 yrs of playboy, gym membership. HERS: 100's of Romance novels, 5 yrs of playgirl, 6 cats, gym membership. Best offers, everything must go.

You now have all the tools you need to successfully shop the used market. So many opportunities lie ahead that will excite you and probably amaze you. Here are the steps you need to get started today.

STEP 1: CREATE YOUR WISH LIST

It is a fact that people who write down their goals are more likely to succeed. The Wish List supplied in Appendix B can help you organize your priorities. Read your Wish List daily to help motivate you to take action. Be sure to review your list periodically as your needs and wants change. Start today!

STEP 2: PREPARE YOURSELF FOR SUCCESS

Address any issues that you fear about the used market. If you do have concerns, the only way to overcome them is to take action. Choose an item off of your Wish List and learn everything you can about models, features, service records and prices. The more you learn, the less fear you will have.

STEP 3: FIND THE ITEM

Use the many places suggested like the Internet, classified ads, bulletin boards, etc. Locate the advertisements and call the sellers using the Buyer Worksheet to organize the information. There are hundreds of deals just waiting to be found in your area.

STEP 4: MAKE THE DEAL

Once you telephone the seller and find the item you want, it's time to make the deal. Use the tips you have learned to determine the seller's motivation (Chapter Six) and close the deal (Chapter Seven).

Start today and enjoy the purchasing power of the used market. With the techniques you have learned, you can avoid depreciation, feel more confident and accumulate wealth and savings. This is a fun and rewarding experience that can bring you both pride and enjoyment.

Get started today and enjoy your success!

Valuable

Resources

APPENDIX

INTERNET CLASSIFIED ADS

As everyone knows, the Internet has become the fastest growing industry of our time. Almost everything is available at the touch of a mouse button, offering a tremendous opportunity for those shopping in the used market.

Many local newspapers are available online with the capabilities to search the classified ad section in minutes. Check with your local paper to see if they are online, or search for their name at one of the many search engines.

If you surf the World Wide Web, you will find numerous sites that deal in national classified ads. However, many of them include advertisements of dealers, retailers and other advertisers rather than simply individual advertisements. Here are a few that have gained popularity and can offer you good results:

Excite Classifieds and Auctions
Web Address: www.classifieds2000.com

Previously known as Classifieds2000, this is a national database of classified ads. It provides free private party classified ads and online auctions.

Yahoo Classifieds and Auctions
Web Address: classifieds.yahoo.com

Yahoo offers a national database of classifieds ads available for viewing by region. All classified ads and online auctions are free.

The Bargain News
Web Address: www.bargainnews.com

This is the online site of the weekly publication covering all of Connecticut, southern Rhode Island, southwestern Massachusetts, and neighboring New York counties. The publication is dedicated to classified advertising and the online version offers a "Super Fast Bargain Search tool."

The Online Network of Pennysavers
Web Address: www.pennysaver.net

This site offers a nationwide network of pennysavers categorized by state, making it is easy to find the publications in your area.

CONSUMER REVIEWS OF PRODUCTS

There are publications that can offer valuable insight into history
or repair trends on a particular product. It is best to consult your
local library or bookstore to find a book that reviews the item you
are interested in purchasing. Here are few places to begin.

Consumer Reports
Web Address: www.consumerreports.org

Consumer Reports is a nonprofit agency that tests consumer
products. Their publication is available in several formats: a
monthly magazine, a year in review and online. They review and
supply information on all kinds of household products, automobiles, tools, appliances, safety equipment and much more. In
addition their web sight offers a wealth of information on products, current manufacturer recalls, safety issues and consumer
protection. Before venturing out to look at an item for sale, check
Consumer Reports for their analysis on repairs, options, and
brand name differences.

Carfax® Vehicle History Service
Web Address: www.carfax.com

Carfax® collects information from numerous sources to provide
vehicle history information. Their database has over 750 million
vehicle history records that are updated monthly from sources
which include state registration records, auto auctions, salvage
auctions, Canadian DMV and rental/lease car companies. You
can find out information on a preowned car just from the VIN
(Vehicle Identification Number). This company charges a fee for
these services, but does offer a free "lemon check."

PRICING GUIDES

Pricing guides are a great source of information for the used market. Your local library and bookstores are filled with hundreds of guides on many different items such as cars, boats, stamps, coins, china, clocks, antiques, toys, furniture, collectibles and more. Listed below are some of the more popular pricing guides used today.

Kelley Blue Book
Web Address: www.kbb.com
Email: Kelley@kbb.com

Kelley offers several blue books on new and preowned cars, motorcycles, motor homes and manufactured housing. The information is updated two to six times per year. Their web site offers new car, preowned car and motorcycle pricing.

Edmund's® Publications Corp.
P.O. Box 18827
Beverly Hills, CA 90209-4827
Web Address: www.edmunds.com
Email: editor@edmunds.com

Edmund's® guide offers information and pricing on new and preowned automobiles. Their web site gives consumer information related to incentives and rebates, expert analysis, information about the auto world, automobile reviews and new car pricing. Their publication is available in libraries, bookstores and online.

National Automobile Dealers Association (N.A.D.A.)
8400 Westpark Drive
McLean, VA 22102
Telephone: 703-821-7000
Web Address: www.nada.org
Email: nada@nada.org

NADA offers a wealth of information and pricing on automobiles, marine equipment, recreational vehicles, motorcycles, snowmobiles and personal watercraft. The company collects data from more than 150,000 retail sales each month as well as 350,000 actual sales transactions from auctions nationwide. The information is evaluated along with other variables like market and economic trends, environmental concerns and government changes. Their publications are available in libraries, bookstores and many banks where it is used to determine the book value on a car loan. Issues are updated approximately every two weeks.

Orion Research Corporation
14555 N. Scottsdale Road, Suite #330
Scottsdale, AZ 85254
Telephone: 1-800-844-0759
Fax: 602-951-1117
Web Address: www.bluebook.com

Orion Blue Book offers appraisals and pricing guides on audio equipment, cameras, computers, copiers, guitar and musical instruments, guns, professional sound equipment, power tools, video and television equipment and other collectibles. Their pricing guide is available in bookstores, on diskette or CD-ROM. Appraisals are offered over the Internet.

Blue Book Publications, Inc.
Web Address: www.bluebookinc.com
Email: bluebook@bluebookinc.com
Telephone: 1-800-877-4867

Blue Book Publications specializes in pricing and reference guides for collectors covering merchandise such as guns, billiards, electric and acoustic guitars, pool cues and more. Publications can be ordered online or by telephone.

Forms

WISH LIST

PRIORITY   I WISH I HAD / I NEED TO REPLACE...

_____	_____
_____	_____
_____	_____
_____	_____
_____	_____
_____	_____
_____	_____
_____	_____
_____	_____
_____	_____
_____	_____
_____	_____
_____	_____
_____	_____
_____	_____
_____	_____

BUYER WORKSHEET

DATE

FOUND AD IN

SELLER'S NAME

ADDRESS

TELEPHONE NO.

PRODUCT MAKE/MODEL

YEAR/AGE

ASKING PRICE

BEST PRICE

☐ NEGOTIABLE

OTHER

CONDITION/USE

REPAIRS/REPLACEMENT PARTS

DIRECTIONS

BILL OF SALE

(GENERAL)

SELLER (OWNER)	NAME	
	ADDRESS	
	CITY, STATE, ZIP	
PURCHASER	NAME	
	ADDRESS	
	CITY, STATE, ZIP	
SELLING PRICE	$	The owner of the item described below hereby transfers ownership to the purchaser in consideration of the selling price.
DESCRIPTION		
SIGNATURE	I declare that the information provided above is true to the best of my knowledge and belief.	SIGNATURE OF SELLER DATE

BILL OF SALE

(MOTOR VEHICLE)

SELLER (OWNER)	NAME	
	ADDRESS	
	CITY, STATE, ZIP	
PURCHASER	NAME	
	ADDRESS	
	CITY, STATE, ZIP	
SELLING PRICE	$	The owner of this motor vehicle described below hereby transfers ownership to the purchaser in consideration of the selling price.
DESCRIPTION	YEAR	MAKE	MODEL
	VEHICLE IDENTIFICATION NUMBER	OTHER
SIGNATURE	I declare that the information provided above is true to the best of my knowledge and belief.	
	SIGNATURE OF SELLER	DATE

BILL OF SALE

(VESSEL)

SELLER (OWNER)	NAME		
	ADDRESS		
	CITY, STATE, ZIP		
PURCHASER	NAME		
	ADDRESS		
	CITY, STATE, ZIP		
SELLING PRICE	$	The owner of this vessel described below hereby transfers ownership to the purchaser in consideration of the selling price.	
DESCRIPTION	YEAR	MAKE	LENGTH	MODEL
	HULL I.D. NUMBER	OTHER	
SIGNATURE	I declare that the information provided above is true to the best of my knowledge and belief.	SIGNATURE OF SELLER	DATE

Glossary

Bank Check
A secured check issued by a financial institution

Barter
To trade by exchanging goods or services without using money

Bill of Sale
A document stating the buyer took ownership of an item

Buy
To acquire by payment or exchange

Classified Advertising
A categorized listing of products for sale

Deposit
Money given as a down payment

Depreciation
Decrease in value of property due to wear, time, obsolescence
or market demand

Durable Good
Items usable for a relatively long period of time such as
machinery, automobiles or household appliances

Failure
The time when a product is no longer usable

Fair Market Value
The average value of a product based on market demand

Great Deal
A good or service purchased below fair market value

Hidden Costs
The fees associated with the purchase of a product that are not easily identified by the purchaser

Nonrecoverable Cost
Money paid that can not be recovered

Owner
Person who has the legal ownership of a good or service

Planned Obsolescence
The planning of a time when a product will no longer be in use

Pricing Guide
A publication defining fair market value for products

Product Life Cycle
The life of a product from the time of purchase to the time of failure

Salvage Value
The recoverable price of a product after its failure point

Sell
To give ownership to another in exchange for money

Seller
Person offering goods or services for sale

Title
A legal document establishing ownership of property

Upgrade
To sell or trade an item for one of higher value or quality

Used Market
Marketplace consisting of preowned merchandise

Vehicle Identification Number (VIN)
Unique series of digits used to identify a vehicle

Warranty
A guarantee of the integrity on a product

Win/win Negotiating
A deal in which both buyer and seller are satisfied with the terms

Index

"50% OFF" IS ONLINE

WE WANT TO HEAR FROM YOU!

visit us on the web at
www.50offdeals.com

email: comments@50offdeals.com

✓ What Great Deals have you made? Email us your story.

✓ Send us your comments on the book. What did you enjoy most? What chapters were most helpful?

If you do not have Internet access yet,
send your comments to:

TLC Publishing
Comments
P.O. Box 8246
New Fairfield, CT 06812

Notes

Notes

Notes

FREE

WEB GUIDE

An easy to use Web Guide
to more than 2000 FREE sites offering:

✓ **FREE** Pricing Guides

✓ **FREE** Local Newspapers and Classified Ads

✓ **FREE** Internet Access (No setup or monthly fees)

✓ Online Auctions

✓ Important Consumer Information

   ...and more

License Agreement